Bleeding Roses

by Emeri Watson

emeri watson

content warning:
this book contains some strong adult themes.

Dedication

This book is dedicated to my sister, Dani. Thank you for always encouraging me to write and being the only one who took my poetry seriously. I owe you.

emeri watson

emeri watson

Chapter One

emeri watson

Written Before You

i feel as if my life
is divided in two parts

there was before you
and after you

you were the seismic event
that split my continents in pieces

-looking back

i am sick of the way
everyone leaves me
and sets me down
when i am no longer
convenient

some mistakes
just feel too good
not to make
over and over
again

emeri watson

i wish that i could just look at someone as
perfect as you without automatically looking
at myself and seeing all the ways i fall short
of the ideal you set

how can you not see
that the way you put me
down
just to make yourself
feel better
hurts me?

emeri watson

i am not strong enough
to turn the tables
on you

i am so sick
of navigating through
the endless jungle
that is this life

why must the memory
of my favorite place
be tainted
with your presence?

i can't believe
i was foolish enough
to share something so special
with someone
who didn't deserve it

emeri watson

do you not see
that when you drink so much
and get so angry
you leave lasting scars
on our small hearts?

you cannot discover yourself
until you get the courage
to look within
unafraid
of not liking
what you might find

promises are about as valuable as pennies
and just as abundant, if not more so

they say
that abused children
either become like
their abusers
or become the opposite

i wonder which one i will be
as i look back on my life

i hope that i have the strength
to drown
all the parts of me
that come from you

i will never let you treat me
like
an afterthought
ever again

emeri watson

i keep driving
as far as i can go
deep into the night

if only
i could escape my problems
as easily as i
can drive away
from what i know

-drive away

show me you love me
by paying attention
to what i share with you

i wonder
if you miss me
like I miss you

i wonder
if i will ever be
close enough
to anyone else

to want to share
my favorite book
with them

emeri watson

i don't think you understand
that though these words you say
mean nothing to you

to me

they are like boulders
flung into a small pond
making enormous waves

-*you don't understand the ways you hurt me*

of all the nights
of not being able to sleep
this one
hurts the worst
because i cannot
get you
off my mind

-*you on my mind*

emeri watson

rekindling
old flames
a bitter pasttime

how am i supposed
to have a healthy relationship
when my only role models
have fallen apart
so bitterly?

everything looked
more beautiful
with you

sometimes i lose track
of what's real
between us
and what's just the product
of my fantasy

i never want to lose sight
of my hatred
for everything you are
lest i slowly become
even a tiny fraction
of you

fake love
will have you questioning
the intentions
of everyone
who claims to love you

-*fake love*

emeri watson

one day
i hope
that i will see
that all of this pain
was leading to something

-trials of pain

i will never stop hating you
for the way
you make me question
whether everyone
who comes after you
is lying to me
like you were

-*cycle of mistrust*

i am sick
of being judged
by people
who don't understand me

i wish that i could
go back in time
and tell myself
how much pain i would save myself from
if i just
avoided
meeting you

emeri watson

Chapter Two

emeri watson

Written While We Were Still In Love

you came up to me
as i was sitting there
at the bar

i don't know why i thought
that just because
you were beautiful
on the outside
you would be beautiful
on the inside
too

he promised a future
she trusted him

the only good advice
my mother ever gave me
was to never waste time
on men
you meet in bars

emeri watson

you told me i was beautiful
and your words
lit my heart aflame

i don't know
if i love or hate
the way
you make me feel
like everything
is coming
out of focus

emeri watson

i have a hard time believing
that anyone has good intentions
least of all tall, dark-haired men
with too much charm
for their own good

handsome men
are a bad habit
i just cannot quit

you asked me about myself
and actually listened to what i said
something i hadn't felt
in such a long time

you seduced me with your attention
and your steely gaze

emeri watson

i wish that i could quiet
the cynic
within myself
and just give myself over
to loving without reservation

the hardest part of life
is just knowing
what decision to make
in the chaos of the moment

i know that i should hold myself back
and not allow
my desires
to rise to the surface

but that gets harder and harder
by the minute

you asked me
to go home with you
just to watch something
and see what happened

no commitment to do anything
just spontaneous freedom

against my better judgement
i said yes

are you going to toss me aside
at the first moment
you want someone else?

i found myself feeling things
with you…

a strength of desire
i had never felt before

emeri watson

i gave myself to you
in that small twin-sized bed

you took me
and i let you have me

you were only my second time
but you were nothing like the first

you were better
in every way

emeri watson

i never imagined that sex
could be better
than the awkward, silent kind
i had had before
where it was all about him

emeri watson

you worked magic
beneath those sheets

part of me
wants to question
how you got so experienced
and what that means
to me

the other part of me
is too busy enjoying it
to care

you turned the quiet, nerdy girl into a
screamer

-*you worked magic with those fingers*

emeri watson

we stayed up all night
talking about everything
that crossed our minds

i love the way
you do more
than just listen to me

you make me
feel heard

i am sorry for the way
i trail off mid-sentence
sometimes

it's just the way
you look at me
you make me feel
so alive

-beautiful dream

you traced your fingers
along my cheek
and cupped your hands
around my face
as you leaned in
to kiss me

-better than i dreamed it

i feel so vulnerable
in this moment
laying next to you

-i hope my secrets don't spill out

i don't know when
we fell asleep
or who dozed off first

i just remember
waking up next to you
and hoping
this wouldn't end
with the rising sun

-*hold me longer*

emeri watson

Chapter Three

emeri watson

Written When You Left Me

i can't help but notice
that your texts
have gotten less and less frequent
and your attention
seems as rare
as water in a desert
these days

-*growing distant*

what was it about me
that's just not worth it to you?
am i too clingy?
too damaged?

all i want
is to love you
but you
don't seem to want that

a woman
should never have to question
whether a man
loves her
or not

i see her name
popping up on your phone
more and more these days

i can't help but wonder
if there's some correlation
between that
and the way
you seem
to be fading away from me

i wonder
are you beginning
to chose someone else
over me?

more and more often
i am withdrawing to my safe place
among these cushions
and books
against the windowsill

emeri watson

i've been thinking too much
lately

i can't keep you
off my mind

are you trying
to push me away?

or am i
just reading into things?

emeri watson

i shouldn't have to wonder
whether you still
have any interest in me

i am getting sick
of waking up each morning
with no idea
whether you
will be
hot
or
cold
today

do you really love me
or did you just
want to use me
for a few nights?

i have to question how much something like
this is worth saving. maybe it's some kind of
a fallacy. the idea that there is something of
value here.

i can't help but think that maybe the way
you make me question whether or not it's
worth it is actually driving me towards the
conclusion that it is worth it.

i don't know. i don't know anything. you
make everything so fuzzy and confusing and
frustrating. maybe that's exactly what you
want.

i spent far too much
of my time
questioning whether you still loved me
when i could have been
moving on
to better things

a woman
should never have to lay in bed at night
lonely
wondering
if she is loved

love is not love
without a sense of security

emeri watson

there is a fire building in my bones
slowly growing larger by the day
a growing sense of revenge

be careful
or the way you treat me
will come back to haunt you

pull me out of my shell
help me feel alive
i feel stuck in place
unable to move
incapable of getting beyond
my own self

it feels more and more
like i am falling
beneath the surface
of the waves

drowning
into the abyss
of sadness
reaching out
with both hands

you are above me
but you don't reach out
to save me

i am helpless
sinking
beneath the waves

losing you
was bad enough
but it hurt all the more
that i never saw it coming

you hurt me in ways
i can't even describe
and you have the nerve
to ask me
if we can be friends again?

you
drove me away
like some minor inconvenience
without so much courtesy
as you would give
a fly
to be swatted
out of the air

now
i am beginning to see
why
you never trusted me

you just knew
that you couldn't be trusted
and so you projected your flaws
onto me

love can transport us
to another place
a transcendence
above the heavens

but heartbreak
slams us back
to the ground
leaving us more broken
than before

emeri watson

i know
that you
are ultimately
nothing more
than a stepping stone
to something better
something real

emeri watson

i want to pack my bags
flee this city
start a new life
somewhere new

i wonder
if you ever cried for me
the way
i cried
for you

you left me with a fire in my bones
ready to burn down the world

never again will i settle
for half-hearted life
or half-hearted love

dear god
put back together
the shattered pieces
of my heart

it hurts to be broken
longing
to feel whole again

you taught me
to never accept
someone
who treats me
the way
you treat me

i despise you

i deserve to hate you
after what you did to me

i don't owe you my love
or affection

you get exactly what you deserve
and that
is my hatred

-fuck you

i want to run into you
in a decade or so
and force you to see
how much better i am
without you

while you
are in misery
shackled
to someone who never
loved you

i want to bury you
beneath the earth
with no way back
to the surface

i am not ashamed
of the rage i feel
towards you

you deserve
every ounce
of it

emeri watson

i was never enough for you
and I have
to come to terms
with that fact

life is too short
to be weighed down
by thoughts of you

emeri watson

Chapter Four

---

emeri watson

Written When I Finally Got Over You

finally
the thoughts of you
have finally stopped
pervading my mind
at every
waking hour

emeri watson

i can't blame
everything that happened
on you

but i am sick and tired
of blaming it all
on myself

life doesn't always move
in the direction we want it to
and accepting that
is the first step
to happiness

do not forget
the goddess you are
deep within

do not allow
him
to define
your self worth

you are more valuable
than he can possibly see

i think women
should be allowed
to enjoy sex
as much as men do
without having
to feel guilty for it

you deserve someone
who won't stop treating you right
when things get difficult

one day
you will wake up
next to the person
you love most
in the world
and feel complete

do not forget
that one day
all of these bad romances
will have taught you
what true love
is supposed to look like

do not forget
that one day
everything
will fall
into place

today
i am determined
to begin the process
of healing

i can't pretend
that i don't still
think about you
sometimes

but it happens
less and less
these days

-progress

looking for love
in bars
was the mistake
that led to you

so tonight
i'm not looking for love

i'm looking for a one night stand
to help me
get over
you

emeri watson

sexually attractive men
are a dime a dozen

so choose one
who will hold your heart gently
and not disappoint you

hold your worries
against your chest
then raise them
to the sky
and let them go

-release

you
showed me
that my first instincts
about people
are always right

emeri watson

never lower your standards
to be with someone

you
are worth
far more
than to be
just another trophy
of a man
who doesn't give a shit
about anything
but your body

-do not let him make you his trophy

i have grown more comfortable
lately
demanding
to receive
what i deserve

emeri watson

i get so lost
in my own thoughts
sometimes

it's hard to remember
to just relax
and take it slowly

i will drown
the memories of your touch
in the arms
of a new man

emeri watson

do not make the mistake
of taking life
too seriously

remember to laugh
and do not let your sorrows
hold you down
for too long

-do not forget the light

if i ever find someone
who can handle me
on my worst days

i know that i will have found
a diamond
in the rough

emeri watson

i am finally
over you.

a new chapter
in my life
has begun

and i
could not
be happier
to let go
of us

i find my peace
in my favorite place
by the stream
outside of town
where everything feels
slow

never be afraid
to be alone
with your own thoughts

that
is where
you discover
who you are

we are battling
against the clock
trying to shove
a lifetime of achievements
into our youth

emeri watson

to be soft
is not the same
as to be weak

you mistook my kindness
for weakness
and exploited it
for your own gain

but i will not
let that
make me
lose my kindness

because that
would mean
you win

-*kindness*

i don't have
all the answers
but i do have
the hope
that in the end
everything
will work out
for the best

you tried
to hit me up
again

i am proud of myself
for laughing
instead of crying

you
have no power
over me
anymore

-*no power*

emeri watson

find someone
whose love
does not demand
that you become
less
of who you are
to please them

-true love does not subtract from who you
are

now she
is feeling free
as a bird
on the breeze

no thanks
to you

-*over you*

love
requires sacrifice
but not
about
who you are
as a person

find someone
who doesn't want
to change you

if finding myself
means losing you
that is a sacrifice
i am willing to make

-chose yourself first

emeri watson

my expectations
for love
have never been higher

i will never settle
for as little
as i did with you
ever again

i hope your read this book
and finally understand
all the ways
you hurt me

i have learned
never to doubt
my intuition

sometimes you just know
about people

it's a gut feeling
you just have to trust

-intuition

i vow to be
a little more careful
with the words 'i love you'

i gave them to you
all too soon

never be afraid
to prioritize
yourself

-self love

despite your best efforts
i am here
happy
finally free
from the scars
you gave me

i hope
you know
that you failed

people will take
everything
you are willing
to give up

-stay strong

you had turned love
into a negative word

my heart
was bleeding roses

but now
love
does not hurt
as much as it did
before

emeri watson

i wonder if you hear
the breeze in the night
rustling against the trees
and think of me

my heart had bled
the deep red of roses
but now i have healed
and the scars
no longer hurt
like they used to

i am ready
to find
a love
that heals

-*roses*

emeri watson

The End

Thank you for reading.

Bleeding Roses

Bleeding Roses is a book of poetry about how it feels to fall in love and the heartbreak that comes after. it is a journey from pain to healing, from a place of brokenness to a new place of healing.

86282819R00095

Made in the USA
San Bernardino, CA
27 August 2018